The Fox and the Stork
with
The Man, His Son and theDonkey

Illustrated by Val Biro

Award Publications Limited

Stork and Fox were good friends. But Fox was always playing tricks on poor Stork.

One day Fox invited Stork to dinner. The table was laid with bowls full of delicious soup, but there were no spoons.

Fox easily lapped up the soup, but poor Stork could not eat any because of her long beak.

Stork loved her friend dearly, but she was tired of his tricks. So she invited him to dinner.

Stork cooked Fox his favourite meal and she served it in two tall jugs.

Fox could not get his nose into his jug to reach the tasty food. But Stork could reach it easily.

So Stork finished both meals and Fox went hungry.

Clever Stork had taught Fox a lesson. He stopped playing tricks on his dear friend.

The Man, His Son and the Donkey

One day a man and his son set off to take their donkey to the market to sell him.

The man wanted the donkey to look fit and well, so the man and his son did not ride the donkey to the market.

Along the way they passed some old women. "Shame on you! You should let the young boy ride the donkey!" the women said.

The man lifted his son on to the donkey's back. He did not want the women to think he did not care for his son.

Further on they came across three old men. "Shame on you, boy! You should let your poor father ride the donkey!" said the men.

The son wanted to please the old men, so he did as he was told. The son walked and let his father ride the donkey.

Then they met three farmers. "A donkey can carry two people. You should both ride it!" the farmers said.

The man did not want the farmers to think that he was foolish. So he and his son both rode the donkey.

When they passed a village, some children shouted to them, "Your donkey is tired. Let him have a ride!"

The man and his son could not carry the donkey on their backs.

But they wanted to please the children, so they tied the donkey onto a pole and carried him like that.

When they got to the market, everyone laughed at the man and his son as they carried their donkey over the stone bridge.

"That donkey must be lame!" shouted a passerby. "Why else would they carry him?"

The man was sad when he heard this. "No one will buy our donkey now," he thought.

Suddenly, the donkey kicked and the pole broke. The man, his son and the donkey all fell into the river.

Splash! Everyone laughed. The man and his son had tried to please everyone, but in the end they had pleased no one.